SCOOTER
CRAZY

They came gliding out of the mist. Eight figures riding state-of-the-art scooters.

And we just stood there – wide-eyed. Our jaws hanging open as they started popping tricks, stunts and moves like you wouldn't believe.

Mind-blowing grabs, truly rad grinds, totally incredible spins, twists, and plants...

Then they were gone.

And no one else could say for sure if they were real.

Except for me.

I knew.

Coz I found the backpack.

It was stamped with the logo STREETSTYLER, and inside was page after page after page of scribbled notes. Some in languages I still don't understand. Some with diagrams for tricks no human being could possibly do. Awesome stuff.

No one has seen the Streetstylers since.

It's time their skills were passed on...

THE ULTIMATE GUIDE

BEN SHARPE

Illustrated by Paul Cemmick

The Chicken House

An Egmont joint venture

This one's for the three planks:
**Dudley, Toilet Boy & Corporate Kev
CHEESE!**

From the Publisher:
Thank you Janet and Mandy!

First published in Great Britain in 2000
by The Chicken House, 2 Palmer Street, Frome,
Somerset BA11 1DS

Copyright © The Chicken House 2000
Text by Ben Sharpe
Illustration copyright © Paul Cemmick 2000

ISBN 1 903434 21 1

British Library Cataloguing in Publication data available.
Library of Congress Cataloging in Publication data available.

Cover and text design by Mandy Sherliker
Printed and bound in Great Britain by Cox & Wyman

Contents

Your attention please!

Riding scooters is fun and exciting; riding them well requires practice and skill! Following the safety guidelines in this book may help minimize any injury, but the use of appropriate safety equipment is strongly recommended.

You've just got your hands on the ultimate guide to everything you could ever want to know about scooters. Whether you're:

◆ A total beginner looking to buy your first scoot.
◆ A push'n'glide expert after some rad new tricks.
◆ Or, just wanting to find out more about the coolest, shiniest, urban-funkiest way to ride the streets...
    ...then you are definitely in the right place!

We are gonna guide you through everything from choosing your first scooter, to perfecting the kind of killer stunts and moves that'll get all your friends drooling.

So check out chapters one and two right now, and let's get down to some serious streetsurfing! ARRROOOOOOOOOOOOW!!!!

Before we leap on in, we need to be sure that we're all talking about the same kind of scooters here...

What Streetstyler is not gonna talk about is motorized minipeds. Not to say they aren't cool. They most definitely are. It's just that they're the subject for another book. Besides, most of us aren't gonna be driving for a good while yet, right? And, anyhow, we all know deep down that there ain't no power like push-power. Especially when it comes to seriously impressing your mates and being cool to the environment.

What we *are* talking is:
- **FOOT-PROPELLED**
- **SINGLE RIDER** (unless you're crazy enough to try piggy-backing!)
- **LIGHTWEIGHT SPEED & TRICK MACHINES**
- **THE FASTEST AND GROOVIEST** way to get from A to B and to any other spots in between.

Why walk somewhere in ten minutes when you can *gliiiiiiiiiiiiiiiiiiiiide* there in three?! And look mega mega cool while you're doing it!

We *did* already tell you about the *cool*

factor, right...?

We didn't?

Well, take it from the Streetstyler – you *will* look sooooo cool. Oh boy... You WILL!

THE VIBE

If you don't own a scooter yet, we bet you've seen some around. If not, where *have* you been hiding? Scooters are the hottest craze of this fresh new century, and there's over a million streetsurfers out there just waiting for you to join them.

The Streetstyler still remembers the first time one zipped past us. A bright metallic-silver blur, curving round pedestrians and bouncing off the curbs. We were like, *HELLO!!*

Then the kid riding the scoot jumped off, folded it in one quick motion and headed into school. That *totally* did it for us. We just had to get one! Well, how could we not be impressed with something that moved so fast and could still fold down small enough to fit into a school bag?!

So we bought one ... and were totally *blown away!*

Coz so much about these scooters is totally excellent.

Totally, totally excellent.

FIRST UP

Scooting is super easy to learn. It takes maybe fifteen minutes to get to grips with the basics of push, slide and glide. You just need a tiny bit of brake-control and a little natural balance. Sure, learning tricks and stuff takes a while longer, but the Streetstyler can promise you that after just one session you'll be asphalt-surfing like a pro. Especially if you follow our guidelines in chapter four! SliiiiiilllIDIN'!!!

SECOND POINT

These scooters are truly light. Check the specs in chapter two, if you don't believe us. Even the heaviest are not much more than four kilos. That means you can stuff one in your bag at school, the movies, wherever, and it won't break your arm off while you're carrying it. A double bonus, coz you can grab a bus, train, or whatever and go scoot somewhere new without feeling like you're lugging a ton of metal.

FREEDOM!!

Can you think of any other transport that gives you this much freedom...? Us neither. Try catching a bus with your mountain bike. Or ramming a skateboard in your bag and slipping into double math class... It just ain't gonna happen.

You can use your scooter absolutely anywhere. On the sidewalks, on a track, offroad, in the half-pipe, even through school if you're sly enough. And you can have a whole load of fun whether you're with your mates, or just hanging on your own. Scooters are great for cruising, racing, or freestyle trickery. Especially when you've grabbed a few hours' practice without anyone else knowing. Not that anyone in the Streetstyler posse would be that sneaky...

Oh, wait.
We have to do the introductions.
These are the guys the
Streetstyler hangs with, and
we thought it'd help to have
them along on this book, coz
they probably know some
stuff we don't...

Nah.
Well ... maybe just a little.

name:
David Lions
age: 9

scooter type: none yet.
don't know what to get.

likes: just want to ride.

specialist skills: none yet!!!

top tip: don't tell your mom
how much decent scooters
cost till you get to the shop.

name: Phantom Ollie
age: 12

scooter type: Micro Pro and Ciro.

likes: offroading and cool tricks.

specialist skills: ollies and back-wheel jumps.

top tip: don't practice TailWhips indoors.

name: KT_90
age: 10

scooter type: Micro Classic.

likes: scooting around town with my friends.

specialist skills: curb bouncing. It is hard!!!!!

top tip: stunts are for geeks!!!!

name: RikFly
age: 11

scooter type: Kick Board, and Razor MS 130 B.

likes: blowing your minds with serious moves and air!

specialist skills: everything.

top tip: watch me and learn!

name: Trinity
age: 11

scooter type: a PushPed.

likes: racing with my brothers.

specialist skills: I don't know!!!!

top tip: don't always kick with the same foot. You get less tired.

name: Chloe
age: 12
scooter type: Micro Air flex (and my brother's Xootr).
likes: skateparks.
specialist skills: grinds and wall-rides.
top tip: if you don't get a trick dialed straight off, just keep on trying.

Streetstyler knows you will be in truly good hands listening to these guys. Especially when Chloe talks. That doesn't happen often but when it does, you really want to pay attention. If there's a trick or stunt for any kind of scoot that Chloe can't do 100 percent perfectly, Streetstyler hasn't heard of it. She is one cool cat.

Not like Richard Flynn (aka RikFly). He's not half the rider he thinks he is. Thinks he can do a 360° TailWhip, but the Streetstyler ain't never even seen him complete a decent Ollie. You have been warned!

And if, after meeting geek-boy Rik, you need a little reassurance that scooters are as cool as the Streetstyler keeps telling you, then check out how many MAJOR celebs we've bumped into while surfing those sidewalks...

SHINE LIKE STARS

Jake Lloyd, Jon Bon Jovi and that sporty Mel C have all been seen giving it some serious scoot. And those extreme sports stars Eric Koston, Dave Mayhew, and Tony Hawk have all been checking out the possibilities for this rad new trick-discipline. Up for trying a 900° on one of these, Tony?!

Just the other day Britney Spears tried to cut us up on a Kickboard! We sorted her though. No one messes with the Streetstyler. Unless it's Maurice Greene. That dude is as quick on one leg as he is on two! Rik was actually dumb enough to challenge him to a circuit race. We have *never* seen anyone so shamefully flamed. The Streetstyler doesn't get embarrassed but right then we felt like hanging up our Scoot.

I, er ... had a bad leg that day!

The Streetstyler posse have also clocked Robbie Williams, Sarah Michelle Gellar, Alicia Silverstone and those big rock dudes from Creed, all getting down to some serious push'n'glide action. No – not all together! Though can you imagine the race those guys would've had? Streetstyler's money would definitely have been on those Creed boys – did you see the moves they were pulling in their video?!

Trinity nearly had her toes sliced off in New York City by the lovely Jennifer Lopez, who was off to do a photo shoot. And KT_90 spotted Mickey and Minnie scooting round Disney World.

We even hear rumors that Brian from Westlife has blown out his chauffeur before, just coz he can't get enough of asphalt-surfing!

But it's not just celebs who're bagging

these scoots. The guys who developed *Toy Story 2* are famous for surfing around their offices on 'em, and loads of suity business-dudes have started push-powering to work. Streetstyler's not too sure we would want to scoot in a suit (check out some better combos in chapter four!) but respect to them for at least trying not to be totally boring.

And...

I think we get the point, Streetstyler!

Yeah. Who cares about celebs anyway!

Right. Er... All we were trying to tell you is that scooting is *definitely* hot. Fact.

And it's gonna keep getting bigger and bigger.

So, read right on, and let the Streetstyler help match you up with your ideal street machine...

Can You Fill Me In?

There's Razors, Kickboards, Ninjas, Ciros, Xootrs, City Sticks, Pushpeds and...

Whoaaaaaaaaaaa! Hold up!

No matter what anyone tries to tell you, buying your first scooter is really simple. Especially if you listen to the advice of the Streetstyler!

If you're a first-timer, you don't want to worry too much about add-ons and accessories. As long as you buy a decent brand, all the essentials you need to get street-surfing will be built-in.

How do you know which brands are good?

Well!! Heh heh heh. Never let it be said that the Streetstyler likes to dish dirt, *but* if a scoot doesn't have most of the stuff we talk about below, then it's a real **GLOPPER**!

Every good-quality ride should have this stuff. Minimum!

* A small, easily folded frame.
* A telescopic steering column.
* An anti-slip deck-mat.
* A minimum of two wheels. (If yours has

less than two, some shop-dude has stitched you up with a unicycle. Not good.)

Strength!

Your scooter should also have a strong frame – either injection-moulded aluminum (like the stuff they use to make jet planes!) or a flexible wood-and-metal composite. That way, as long as you don't park it under a bus, it should stand up to almost anything you can put it through.

Weight!

The next thing you need to check out is weight. Scoots range from around three to four kilos. If it's a heavy model, it should look a lot bigger – like the Xootr. If it's small and *still* heavy, then it's made from a bad material. Leave it! Always pick a scoot that feels comfortable to carry. You want to be floatiiiiin'!

Brake!

You need a good brake too. If someone offers you a scoot without one, just don't even think about it! A proper scoot will have either a moulded rear-foot-brake, or a hand-brake. Either one is cool. The foot-brake may seem a little weird when you first try it, especially if you're used to riding a bike. But, after a few stuttering stops, you will have it dialled.

Safety!

Oh... One more thing before you buy. Ask what kind of safety checks your scoot has been put through. Top brands like Razor bash their test-machines with all kinds of stuff before they approve them as safe. If your scoot has survived being lamped with a metal bar, it's a good bet it'll last through a lot of wipe-outs on the street!!

And that's pretty much it ...

 So how come there are so many different brands?!

A Little Bit Of History

Way, way back in 1996, you could only get two types of scoot – the Razor and the Micro. (And they were basically the same thing!). Then people started to want rides that could do a little more. Like go over bumps without spilling them off! Or grind kerbs. Or speed over dirt. Or whatever.

So the two manufacturers started making different styles of scooter to meet all those different riders' needs. Pretty soon a whole load of other companies started making versions of the perfect street-machine too.

Most scoots still look a lot like those early models. (All the Pushpeds, CitySticks, Ninjas, Zappys, as well as most of the Razors, JD Bugs, and Micros.) Well, hey – it was, and is, a design classic. And Streetstyler reckon that lots of you will choose to buy one in that style coz they are sooooo coooool. But, if you fancy something a little more specialized, here's a few of the really rad rides for you to check out...

The Micro Air-Flex

It may *look* like almost every other scoot. But peer a bit closer and you'll see some really hot stuff.

First up, it has a deck made of wood and glass-fiber. That's a more flexible combination than the usual aluminum type, so it can absorb a lot more jolts and bumps. It makes the scoot a little heavier at the base too. And having a low center of gravity is no bad thing when you're flying down a dirt track.

This baby also has air-filled tires, instead

of the usual resin, and ABEC-5 performance bearings. That means you get a nice smooth ride and a lot of wheel-turns per push.

But all those modifications would be useless if the deck-plate was low to the ground like on most other scooters. The good news? It's not. The ride position is set higher off the floor, so you won't have to avoid every last little stone or branch in your path, you can just scoot right on over them. Giddy UP!!!!!!

Streetstyler's spies say the brake is slightly better too. That's got to be good news if you're giving it some serious off-road action and suddenly there's a tree-stump right up ahead!

Here's its awesome vital stats:

frame:	aluminum
deck:	wood/glass fiber
handlebars:	aluminum
grips:	black foam
wheels:	black air-filled tires 150mm, 80 psi
brake:	rear (friction plate) folded size: 705mm long x 235mm high x 345mm wide

total weight:	3.9kg (varies between models)
max. rider weight:	100kg

Had a wicked time with this. Went over bumps that would have totalled my old scoot!

It's OK, I guess, but only if you want to get dirty. I think my old Micro looks nicer!

The Xootr

The first thing you need to know is that the "x" in "Xootr" is pronounced like the "z" in "zoo." The second important fact is that it's BIG! Especially the ride-board. That's great news if you have huge feet, or like to wear phat sneakers. You will be able to gliiiiiiide with both feet onboard, no problem. It's also cool if you're lazy. Having both feet on the deck means you can scoot longer distances without getting tired!

The Xootr has big wheels too. They're about three times the size of normal skate-wheels, and made of ultra-glide polyurethane (a sort of plastic!). So, not only is the ride very smooth, but each push will take you a long way.

It also has a very hard-wearing frame and backward-angled front-forks. Sounds kind of sciencey, doesn't it? All it means is that the Xootr is tough enough to bounce curbs and pull plenty of tricks and moves. So tough, in fact, that one of their models is literally bullet proof!

The design is awesome too. Streetstyler hears that some of the dudes involved in making it used to build racing cars, so we reckon you will definitely get lots of stares if you ride one. Which is cool (unless you fall in a ditch... when someone you think is cute is watching ... and the ditch is full of mud... Not that anything like that would ever happen to the Streetstyler.

Yeah right!

There are three versions of the Xootr available, but they all come with the same basic stuff. Just give these figures an eyeballing:

frame:	aluminum
deck:	laminated-birch/aluminum /carbon fiber (varies between models)
handlebars:	steel
grips:	foam
wheels:	die-cast aluminum rims and polyurethane tires diameter 180 mm
brake:	rear (with hand lever)
folded size:	790mm long x 240mm high x 320mm wide
handlebar height:	adjustable to 965mm maximum
total weight:	4.5 – 4.8kg (varies between models)
max. rider weight:	114kg

I liked this a lot. The board is big and I could go pretty fast without falling off.

The handlebar brake is cool. All the scooters should have this.

Good wheels and bearings on this. I use my brother's when I want to get somewhere quick. Bit heavy though!

The K2 Kickboard

If you're thinking something a bit strange is going on here, then you're right.

The K2 has no handlebars!

Freaky.

Instead, you get a height-adjustable joystick with a bottom end that is fixed to the deck in a sort of knuckle-joint. Crazy, huh? Maybe. But it does mean you can bend the stick really low, making the K2 great for taking corners at speed. Smooooooooooooooth!

At the stick's *top* end, you get a flexible knob. This means you can steer the scoot easily with one hand which is cool if you're carrying something, and especially coz it makes complicated tricks like grabs a lot simpler. Also, the Streetstyler knows that having less metal in front of you is a big bonus if you wipe-out – there's a whole lot less metal to whack into!

Unlike most scoots, the K2's deck is made from a ply construction. The several layers of wood and carbon-fiber make it pretty springy if you hit uneven ground. The bearings are pretty hot, too. Those ABECs again. Good for long smooth gliiiiiiiiiiiiides...

Kickboards also have an extra wheel at the front. Is this cool? Yep. If you're a nervous beginner, the K2 will give you a nice stable ride. And, if you're a pro, you can execute the tougher tricks more easily coz you can really lean on this scooter. (It's much easier to concentrate on nailing a grind if you know the front end isn't just gonna slide away and land you on your tush!) The extra front wheel means the scoot stands up on its own too. The Streetstyler loves that. We can park it somewhere cool, step away and milk those respectful glances. Oh yeah. Thank you fans. Look. Admire. But, NO touching.

Scope these vital vitals:

frame:	aluminum
deck:	wood/glass fiber
steering rod:	aluminum
wheels:	clear polyurethane 100mm diameter
brake:	rear (friction plate)
folded size:	705mm long x 235mm high x 345mm wide
total weight:	3.2kg
max. rider weight:	100kg

One **cool**-looking scooter!

The pole thing is a bit tricky.

You get some great suspension on this stick. Nice tough board and a real fast brake. Guess I'm saving up again...

Most of these scoots are available at your local toy or sports shop. Those that aren't can be bought online. In fact, Streetstyler thinks that buying on the Net is the best way to pick up a cheeky bargain. (Because they weigh so little, delivery costs are low too.)

But don't forget... Cool new rides are being developed all the time. In fact, Streetstyler hears that Ciro has just gone one stage further than the K2 people and put four wheels on their machine. Funky.

If you **STILL** need more help deciding which scoot is the one for you. We have the answer...

Take the Streetstyler Urban Examination!

Just ask yourself this – are you:

A Speed Freak?

- You want to get where you're going as quick as you can...
- You're always looking for a steeper hill...
- You want to race your mates till the soles burn off your sneakers...

Streetstyler recommends...

Look for a light scooter and be sure to check for decent wheel-bearings. The better the bearing, the more turns you get per foot-push. That means it takes less energy to go farther, faster.

After a little practice, you can get some serious speed.

Streetstyler even hears rumors of hard-core racers getting speeds of close to 30kph! (Though we're not so sure we believe that. Even 5kph feels fast on a scoot!)

An UrbanJoyrider?

- You're the cool kid around town.
- The scooter is just one part of your mega-hip look...
- You like to hang outside trendy shops popping tricks and posing...
- You love the thrill of curb bouncing and zipping past pedestrians...

Streetstyler recommends...

All the top scooters look totally hot, so this comes down to which style you like the most. Streetstyler reckons you can't go wrong with clean, silver lines. Metallic scoots look *extremely* cool when the sun catches them – just make sure you choose one with front suspension if you plan to do any serious trickwork. Or, if you really want to turn heads, the Xootrs and Ciros will definitely get people staring. Don't forget though, whatever scoot you get, there are accessories and individual tweaks you can make to create a totally unique ride. Just check out chapter eight.

An OffRoader?

- You like urban action, but love the thrill of dirt-riding...
- You can't get enough of gliding between trees and bouncing obstacles...
- The tougher the terrain, the better the challenge...

Streetstyler recommends...

There's only one or two machines suited to this kind of scooting right now, but all the main suppliers reckon it's gonna be the next big thing, so you should have a lot more choice soon. An offroad scoot has to have a raised and flexible deck – to help you avoid those cheeky low-lying bumps and stones –

plus decent suspension with air-filled tires to give a smoother ride. Don't even try offroading any other way – your scoot and your body will be toast!

Trickster?

- No curb, wall, railing or staircase is too big a challenge...
- You're only happy pushing that scoot – and yourself! – right to the limit...
- Any day now, you really will perfect that 360° TailWhip...

Streetstyler recommends...

You can do basic tricks with all the scoots. And, if you are a real natural, you'll probably be able to coax out some fairly killer advanced moves too. But, for really impressive-looking stunts, you're gonna need either a machine with a good bunch of add-ons – like a trickbar and grind-plate, or a scooter-skateboard cross-breed, like the Kickboard, which is designed specially for trickwork.

Or do you just wanna hang out...?
- And do a little bit of what you fancy!

Streetstyler recommends...
If you just want to ride and hang, any of the scoots will do the job. Streetstyler's only advice is that you don't need to spend loads of cash on one of the newest models. The cheaper scooters are still way cool. Just be sure you are buying from a decent supplier. Or, if you're getting one second hand, make sure the seller is someone you trust!!

Because scooting is so trendy right now, some naughty companies have been making bad fakes of the decent brands. You may save a little cash getting a dodgy scoot, but you are not gonna be happy if it dismantles itself while you're cornering at speed! Streetstyler has seen that happen once too often.

Get out there and grab yourself an asphalt-surfer, and we'll see you again in chapter four!

OK, Daddios. Listen up. You want to sound cool on the street, right? Then chomp onto the RikFly dictionary of def!

Air Any time you jump or Ollie, you are getting some air. Good scoot riders get big air!

Am This is some of you guys. It's short for amateur. If you practice real hard, you might get to be a pro like me!

Bail When you're in the air, and a trick has gone pear-shaped, you bail – leaping away from the scoot to try for a pain-free landing.

Bombing When you get some serious speed – usually down a big hill.

Burly A big trick with lots of potential for pain if you get it wrong! If you're a scoot rider who gets his thrills from the trickier stunts, you're definitely a Burly.

Bust If you bust a trick, you've got it right! If you get busted, some loser is chasing you off his land!

Carve Pulling off a big, fast, aerial scoot-turn.

Dialed When you get a trick right.

"Dropping" Good idea to shout this if you wipe-out on a crowded skate ramp. "ARG!" works just as well though...

Fakie A backward move – usually with just your rear wheel touching the ground.

Flatspots Clear spots on your wheels where the polyurethane has worn away during a trick.

Fruit Boot One good way to diss in-line skaters!

Funbox Any sort of box – usually a wooden one – that you grind or slide on.

Glopper Someone who has made a really bad clothing decision...

Gnarly When something's totally rad!

Goofy You're goofy-footed if you ride with your left foot at the back.

Grommet Little kid scoot-riders like David. Heh heh heh.

Hang Up Getting your front or rear wheel stuck during a trick. Better get ready to slam! (Also called a Lock.)

Hipper A huge, swollen bruise on the hip. You really *don't* want one of these!

Land To A successfully completed trick!

Mongo You are mongo-footed, or "pushing mongo," if you use your leading foot (the wrong one!) to push.

Mullet Really bad hairstyle. Also known as a Kentucky Waterfall, Hockey Hair, Tennessee Top Hat, Canadian Passport, Unhappy Peacock, or Ape Drape.

HEHEHEHE-HEHEHE!!!!!!
That's you Rik.

KT, I **DON'T** have a mullet!

Old Skool A trick, rider, or pretty much anything else that is old style.

Rad When something totally blows you away!

Ripper A good all-round scooter-rider

Session Any time you get together to scoot with your mates.

Sick When something's totally gnarly!

Sack It If you bail and land with something smashed up between your legs – usually your scoot's steering column – then you've sacked it.

Sketchy Someone who's a little bit weird ... and probably a glopper.

Slam A VERY hard fall.

Snake Someone who cuts you up bad, or steals your line into a trick.

Swellbow The grisly results of falling on your elbow!

Technical (Or Tech) Any trick performed on flat ground or a fairly low ledge, involving plenty of technical skill such as a 360° TailWhip.

Tech Dog A scoot-rider who is really hot at technical tricks.

Tweak Adding a personal touch to a well-known trick.

Bet you never expected to learn a whole new language, huh? And the cool thing is, folks are making up bossin' new phrases all the time, so there's nothing stopping you adding your own faves.

Hey dudes! Got your scoots now? **Cool!** Let's **RIDE!**

Whooooaaaaaaa! Easy tiger! Before you hit the streets you need to get the Streetstyler low-down on scooting safety.

Oh brother!

Rik, dude, you were in hospital **TWO WEEKS** that time you didn't wear your helmet!

Er... OK. Maybe safety is important...

Safety is NOT a dirty word. Take it from the Streetstyler. We've seen the scars.

All the scooter-makers recommend you wear a helmet and pads, even if you're just gonna be scooting around your garden, and the Streetstyler is totally with them on that. There is no way you would be allowed to do your stuff in a skatepark without protection, and riding on the sidewalk ain't no different.

I know what you're thinking though. Am I still gonna look cool on my scooter if I'm wearing crash-protection gear?

Want the simple answer? YES! You will. And this is why:

The top scooter-riders, skaters, and inline-skaters are all sponsored by big sports-companies. They don't want their riders to look like they've gone one-on-one with a gorilla, so they've developed all kinds of trendy-looking safety gear. You can get some truly rad stuff to protect every single part of your body from a mashing. Most of it is color and style-coordinated too. You really don't have to look like your head got stuck inside a Chupa Chup to be safe.

Heads Up!

Stuff your head in a top helmet. There are loads of good brands out there. Razor makes helmets specially for scooter riders Boeri, Roces, and Logic are all worth checking out. Basically anything that meets your country's safety standards is cool.

Pro-Tek-Shun!

Wrist guards are a good idea too. Most times when you fall, your hands automatically shoot out to try and soften the impact. Wearing guards means you are less likely to sprain or snap a wrist. YeooooOOW! And, if you plan on doing some of the advanced tricks we show you later in this book, we seriously recommend you look at getting some knee and elbow guards. Smashing up either of those joints is a REALLY BAD IDEA!!!

What the Streetstyler really can't figure is why anyone *wouldn't* want to wear safeties. Scooting can be a dangerous enough sport anyway. Everyone we know has all the right gear, and they still carry the scars of sidewalk conflict!

Da Bone Yard

My worst? We were doing stair jumps down at the Square. The scoot just came right out from under me as I landed. Scraped all the skin off my knee, ripped my pants and dislocated my little finger. That really hurt! I still jumped the most steps though!

Scratched arm and bruised thumb.

Doing X-Ups at Playstation Park – I went to grab some Cokes, tripped over, and broke my wrist!

Two black eyes, a chipped tooth, a broken nose, a squashed ear, bruises all down my left side, and my clothes torn to pieces.

Wasn't that when your little sister beat you up, Rik?

KT – you're so NOT FUNNY!

Hmmm... If you want to keep scrapes to a minimum, the Streetstyler's six hints for keeping body and scoot together will help:

ONE

Always check over your scoot before you ride it. Make sure all its quick-release switches are in the locked position. Scope out whether any screws or levers have worked loose. Give each of the wheels a good spin to make sure they are all turning freely – and that none of them have got too worn.

One time I forgot to check my handlebars. I pulled an Ollie and the column shot right out of the deck-plate. Was mostly embarrassing, but could have hurt a lot...

Check your safety gear too. If your helmet got damaged last time out, or your pads were torn, get new ones.

And don't trap your fingers when you fold or unfold a scooter. Really hurts!

TWO

Car drivers are your enemy! They never look carefully when they are on the road so you have to do the watching for them. Don't go zipping into a road, or out of your driveway without checking first. The Streetstyler is too young to be going to funerals!

Some kid round my way used to scoot in the road. He got run over and nearly died.

!!! STAY OFF THE ROAD!!!

THREE

Don't ride your scoot in any dumb places. There are loads of paved areas and skateparks around, so you really can stay clear of roads. Also, if you're planning to do tricks, make sure you do them somewhere where you have a good view all around. Doing a stair-jump and totalling your head teacher is not too wise.

I only got suspended for a week...

 And then your Mom grounded your butt for three months!

FOUR

Watch out for bad weather conditions. Scoots aren't really designed for the wet so you need to take things really slow and keep your foot over that brake. And don't even think about riding on icy or oily surfaces!

FIVE

Don't ride your scoot at night unless you've *covered* it in fluro-strips and you're wearing reflective clothing. Scoots don't show up anywhere near as well as bikes, so you need to look extra-extra-visible.

And chill! You can STILL look cool. Bright orange and yellow jackets are soooo in. Or you could get some flashing beads for your hair. Well ... maybe not if you are a guy. Unless you have mullet–hair like Rik!

SIX

Know your limits. If you haven't mastered an Ollie, don't try anything crazy like a Tail-Whip. You need to be able to control the scoot in your sleep first!

And if you ever get into trouble pulling a stunt – jump off! Better to bail while you still can. A few sidewalk scrapes are way better than a full-frontal hug from a brick wall.

Now... Let's surf those streets!!! AROOOOOOOOOOOOW!

Riders On The Storm

There is no big secret to riding a scooter. Everyone's style is a little different and it'll take you a few goes to work out what's most comfortable for you. The Streetstyler's top tip is to start out somewhere quiet. Find a stretch of sidewalk that is flat and straight – and isn't already full of pro riders! And take it SLOW.

Standin'

When you first get on the scooter, place your standing foot (the one you won't be kicking with) at a slight angle near the front of the deck. That'll leave room for the toes of your kicking foot to rest just behind it in between kicks. It also means the heel of your kicking foot will be hovering lightly over the rear brake (if your scoot has one) ready for use.

Kickin'

OK. Now you're ready to ride. Plant your kicking foot on the sidewalk and try for a strong and fluid kick. Looking cool on your scoot is all about gliding, not stamping at the ground in an energy-sapping frenzy. Who wants their friends to see them red-faced and stinky with sweat-patches? Not the Streetstyler. Take it from us, steady, rhythmic kicks are the way to go. And remember to change feet regularly too. Otherwise you'll end up with one leg twice the size of the other!

Plantin'

If you get tired quickly it's coz you're working muscles that don't normally get used a lot. After a couple of days you should start to feel OK. If not, you need to make sure you aren't riding like a dork!

To scoot a long way and still be full of energy, you need to be planting your kick-ing foot down toward the front of the scooter. That way you propel yourself and the machine forward. Your kicking foot should always hit the ground close to the scoot too. If you plant too far away, you'll just un-balance yourself, and end up with a way wobbly ride.

Don't bend your knees too much either. It's another way to waste energy. So is putting too much weight on your kicking foot. Spread your weight across the deck if you want to keep an even balance the whole time you're onboard.

Curbin'

Once you've got kicking under control, try getting up and down curbs without slowing down (or falling off!). This is all about timing. Glide up to the curb and, just as you are about to touch it, put your foot down ready to push. At the same time, lift up your front wheel so that it's resting on top of the curb. And *push*. Simple.

Cornerin'

Now all you need to learn is how to turn. When you're gliding around slowly, this is easy – you just move the handlebars! But when you're really zipping along, you've gotta be a bit more sly. As you turn your scoot into the corner, bend toward the handlebars and shift your weight outward so that your body leans into the curve. You don't need to lean much, unless it's a massive corner. Just do enough to stay balanced, and keep some pressure on the brake too. You don't want your scoot's back end to slide away and spin you into a HUGE wipe out! If your scooter does start to slide, either jam on the brake and skid to a halt or ... BAIL OUT! If you *have* to bail, remember to run off the scoot. If you just leap off and try to stand still, your momentum will have you kissing that sidewalk. Nasty!

And that's basically all the skills you need for hanging out, or cruising in town. But to do more advanced scooting, you need a bit more savvy...

SpeedFreakery

To be a genuine and bona fide white-knuckle rider is easy. You just gotta go fast, and finish first! For that, all you really need is good rhythm and a strong kicking action. It's also cool if you can find a pretty steep hill to help build up your speed. If you're racing with your mates, the Streetstyler thinks you should put most of your effort into making a quick start – like a sprinter does. Then settle down into a steady push and gliiiiiiiiide. If you don't get in front from the start, try for a burst of speed as you approach a corner. That way you can cut across the scoot ahead of you and make him chew your dust! OH YEAHH! But *no* pushing or jostling! Scooter riding is NOT a contact sport!!

Remember how you need to lean to get round a corner at speed? If you're a SpeedFreak, you want to get really good at doing this. You want to be a cornering *master*. Some of the best speed-riders lean so far out from their scooters and crouch down so low that they actually have to balance one hand on the road to steady themselves! If you get *that* good, go buy yourself some hard-wearing gloves!

There are two wickedly fast and freaky games you should try out if speed is your bag: Circuits and Road Raging.

Circuits

Find a big flat expanse of concrete. Somewhere like a deserted parking lot. Mark out a course with your bags, coats, chalk, and even street-cones if you can find any. The more stuff you can use, the groovier your circuit will look.

A good course will be sort of circular, like a race-track, so there're plenty of good corners. You should try to find somewhere that is slightly sloped too. That way you will have a downhill section where you can really FLY and an uphill section where you have to push like crazy! Then all you do is decide the number of laps you're gonna race and go! go! GO!

You can race your friends head-on in a massive free-for-all, go one-on-one, or take it in turns doing time-trials against the clock. It's all totally addictive! If your posse all scoot at about the same speed, you can add stuff to the circuit to make it trickier. Try laying a plank of wood across the straight to Ollie over, or putting up a mini ramp. (You'll learn the skills you need to perfect these moves in the tricks section.)

Road Raging

This can be a real hoot. And it's so simple coz you don't need any equipment. It's just you, your friends, and the sidewalks where you live.

All you do is decide where you're gonna race to and what route you're gonna take to get there. The race should last at least a few blocks, and you should try to include as much crazy stuff as possible – like making everyone run up a steep bank, or down some steps (you could try an Ollie there if you were feeling really brave!), or over gravelly ground ... you get the picture. Just use your imagination and try to come up with the trickiest, hairiest course possible. And as soon as you all complete it, challenge yourselves to do it in reverse!!

Offroading

Gliding offroad is like no other kind of scooting. You're gonna encounter all sorts of crazy stuff that you would never meet on the sidewalk. Branches are gonna whip out at you, vines and roots are gonna try to snag your wheels, mud is gonna clog your brakes, and birds and rodents are gonna fling stuff at you. It's a dirty world – and the Streetstyler LOVES it!!!

But, before you head for them thar hills, there are a couple of things you really need to know.

One Offroad scoots are not total all-ter-rain-vehicles. You can't ride through thick mud or piles of heavy leaves. The wheels are just too small. What you can do is ride over gravel, wood chips and pretty much any kind of dry earth, so long as it's not *totally* blitzed with holes.

Two To offroad well, you need to have excellent balance, top braking skills, seriously good slide-control, and lightning reflexes to make sure you stay on that deck! This is coz your scoot will squirm around loads on loose ground.

The trick is to counter-balance. If your scoot flips to the left, lean to the right. If it squirts out to the right, lean the other way. Sometimes this won't straighten out the scooter's front end, but it's better to slide sideways than to eat earth!!!

Three The first few times you try offroad-ing, you're gonna get *really* dirty. The Streetstyler must've come off at least twenty times on our first visit to the forest! If you stop regularly and clean all the gunk off your wheels – especially the back one – you won't spill so often. If you don't clean it, the back wheel can get clogged and stick to the brake. This usually happens at the worst possible moment, and when you will least expect it! The scoot's back end will drag, or lift, and you'll be collecting your arms and legs from a bush. So clean those wheels!

Circuit racing is a little hard offroad – and also less fun, coz it's hard to get the speed you need. But you'll be getting enough thrills from dodging obstacles and making that dirt fly! You can Mud Rage though. The rules are the same as for Road Raging, you just get a heck of a lot muddier and you can dream up even crazier stunts! Come up with a route that includes grinds against logs, or a tree climb, or fence-jumping, or stream-wading, or... Well, you get where we're coming from!!

Oh... One last thing. If you are going offroading somewhere on your own or with friends – tell someone where you're gonna be. The Streetstyler is too busy to organize search parties!

Trickster

If you're a trick-head, we have some great news – you get three whole sections of rad stunts to try out later in the book! But first we want to talk about Horse. This is a cool game to play if you're hanging with a group of friends. And it's simple too – so long as you can do some tricks!

The game starts with one of your posse popping a trick. Then everyone else has a crack at it. Anyone who fails the trick takes the letter "H". Then the next person pops a stunt, and those who can't copy it take an "H", if they did the first stunt, or an "O" if they messed up on the first go round. The winner is the last person in the game not to have spelled out the word. We guess you could use any word, if you liked, but for the Streetstyler posse, it's just always been "Horse."

OK... Up till now you've been scooting somewhere nice and quiet, where no one could see you wiping-out all over the sidewalk or trashing it into those hedges. Now you're ready to go public and hit the streets for real. So you're gonna want to look cool, right...? No sweat. Just heed the advice of our resident fashion queen, KT_90. By the time she's through with you, you are gonna be one funky monkey... Hubba! Hubba!

OK , people. I may not know a lot about tricks. But when it comes to being cool, you better listen up!

Hey! How about me... I got a lot to say about clothes and stuff!

Rik, your mullet does the talking for you. Beat it!

Names

Before you think about what clothes to wear, you should come up with a riding name. Mine's KT_90 coz my name is Katie Morris and I was born in 1990. Cool, huh? If you hang with a group of friends, it's good to have similar nicknames to show that you're all part of the same scooter posse. I mostly scoot with my friends Joseph Kobi (Kobes) and Evelyn Ashton (EV-89). And we are the K Kollective coz of our names and coz we live in Kingston Road.

Your nickname doesn't have to have anything to do with who you are or where you live though. There're these riders called Mingus, Planet, and Prince W. They reckon they are the Deck DJs coz they like music, but we call them the Posh Posse coz they all come from big houses and always wear designer labels!

If you can't think of a groovy name instead for yourself or for your scoot gang, try picking a couple of words from the list below.

CRAZY	RAD	LO
METHOD	DEMON	PLANT
GT	POW	CAT
FIVE-OH	BOMBER	GHOST
PRO	SLAM	SPEED
RAZOR	MONKEY	GIRL
BOY	SILVER	SMOKE
STREET	AIR	ANGEL
DAWG	BEANY	MAGIC
ASPHALT	STAR	FREAK
SURF	TRICKSTER	DIRT
WARRIOR	GLIDER	DUDE

Stick some cool ones together and KT_90 will guarantee you the hippest names in town!

Thinking about the sort of stuff your posse likes to do will help as well. A name like Da Dirt Demons is bossin' if you're offroad freaks like Phantom Ollie and his crowd. But it just makes you sound like gloppers if you're Urban Joyriders. If you hang in town, you need a sleeker name like Silver Gliders or Urban AllStarZ.

Gear

It can be pretty embarrassing if you get caught wearing the wrong kind of outfit for the wrong kind of scooting. But imagine if you wear the wrong sort of clothes altogether... Eek! If you want to escape shame on a MAJOR scale, avoid this stuff like the plague:

Green Wellies When did you last see a cool farmer?!

Dungarees Unless you want to look like a mobile potato sack?

Skin-Tight Cords Just tragic.

Home-Knit Sweaters Thanks Gran but money will be just fine next year.

Ankle Flappers ARG! Someone call the fashion police!!

Platform Shoes Try it. I did. Then I bought a new pair of shoes.

Mullet Hair You mean you've seen Rik and still need a reason?!

Duffel Coats A one-way ticket to over-heating.

Loose-Hanging Jewelry
Looks great till you hang it around the handlebars...

Flip-Flops It's sad, but these are just TOO hard to ride anything in!!

And you know if I catch you wearing ANY of that stuff I'm just gonna have to scoot off in the opposite direction!! So do yourselves a favor and follow *these* freaky fashion and lifestyle hints!

UrbanJoyriders

Fashion-Queen KT always says that there are two things you should never leave home without: rubber-soled shoes and a mini-backpack. Rubber soles, like on my Nikes, help keep your feet on the scooter's deck, and the bag means you can take a drink with you (UrbanJoyriders *always* drink water. Fizzy is for geeks!).

For clothes, you should head for the high street or the mall. As long as what you buy is light and trendy, you will gain max respect. Guys, you should go for dark-dye denims, or narrow-cut urban synthetics, and old-skool style nylon-shirts. I usually wear a mini-dress, shades and a hair-band – as long as it's labels!!

For sounds, your Walkman just *has* to be playing some blissed out urban-noise. From the ultra-cool soul of Craig David or Macy Gray to the huge sprawling sounds of Radiohead and Travis, your choice of music should be as smooooooooooth as your style of scooting!

SpeedFreaks

Trinity says that part of being quick on her scooter is *feeling* quick. Well, she definitely looks speedy to me. I never see her in anything that's not tight, shiny, and just a little bit funky. She gets most of her clothes in sports shops, and is a real fiend for Reebok, Speedo and Adidas. Her brothers all wear shorts, backpacks and sports T-shirts – oh, and of course pads and helmets. They all have sunglasses too. When you're riding fast, it's the only way to stop an eyeful of dirt.

The main thing SpeedFreaks have in common with us Joyriders is footwear. If you're gonna be road-racing on your scoot, you just have to wear lightweight sneakers. Trin has a pair of Nike Turbulence which I'm so jealous of!! She also has a very cool Storm wristwatch with a timer. It totally matches the color of her scoot and is something she just couldn't do without – it's the only thing that stops her brothers cheating!!

And what's Trin's soundtrack for whupping those boys' butts? Anything from the techno rock of the Prodigy to the block-rocking beats of the Chemical Brothers and the Utah Saints. Speedfreaks love any sound with pace and power!

Offroaders

Why anyone would want to get all dirty scooting offroad, I just have no clue. But if you *do*, then normal scoot-gear just won't cut it. You need heavy-duty clothes to

69

protect you from branches, rocks, and brambles – and to save your skin when you wipe-out on that gravelly ter-rain!! Synthetics or thick-weave-denims are the ONLY way to go – and it helps if they're waterproof too. You can pick up some good brands in sports shops – Kickers, McKenzie and Helly Hansen are good strong makes. Or you could try some specialized skate and scoot-wear. Most of their products will be breathable, as well as water-resistant, and hard-wearing.

You'll also need very sturdy footwear. You could probably get away with running shoes on a really dry day, but if you trail your push-foot along the ground to help with cornering, the sole will soon get worn down. Bad news! Instead, go for some kind of hard-soled boots. And don't forget those shades. I don't want anyone crying when they get grit in their eyes!!

Ollie reckons the ideal soundtrack to a day in the wilderness is a mix of the Foo Fighters, Garbage and Rage Against the Machine. This girl would rather stick pins in her ears, but I guess everyone should be allowed to listen to what they like ... even if it is hairy, sweaty, grunt-music...

Tricksters

You will definitely need hard-wearing gear for doing stunts! Chloe is forever having to buy new T-shirts after she gets shredded.

She usually goes for thick, baggy hooded sweatshirts, and pants, and says there's no point spending loads of money on them coz they get wrecked so quickly – especially when your'e trying tricks for the first time. Plus, baggy gear means you can keep your pads on all the time, without

71

getting weird looks on the bus, or where-ever. (And KT_90's number one rule is Only EVER Get Noticed For The Right Reasons!!) Check out companies like Mecca and Triple Soul for real hard-wearing stuff.

If it's hot, then you have to wear a vest-top or T-shirt and knee-length shorts. It's the rules! And the crazier the logo, the greater the respect! But by far the most important thing is the shoes you choose. You need something strong and flexible, with lots of grip and protective strips. The cool thing is that skateboard shoes are great for scooter riders, and there are hundreds of excellent brands making those! If you need somewhere to start, check out Vans, Globe, DCSHOECO, or Chloe's faves: Etnies. Don't buy 'em unless they give you *maximum* comfort!!

Trickster music is all about bringin' da noize!!! Chloe is into some really far out stuff from The Beastie Boys and The Herbalizer to the old-skool sounds of Twisted Sister and the Red Hot Chilli Peppers.

Rik likes Korn, Limp Bizkit and Slip Knot – but we all knew he was a dweeb anyway!

WHAT?!!

Chill out Rik. Some of your choons are cool. And KT's too. It'd be a real downer if everyone liked the same stuff. And no one has to dress a certain way either. Being different is cool. One time we dressed in boiler suits and big furry wigs and scooted all through the precinct. It was a total hoot!

Right. No more messing around. Comi
you now is the first of the Streetstyler's
quick-fire guides to all the top tricks and
totally rad stunts on the PLANET. So grab
your scooter and your safeties, strip off
that backpack and prepare for some hard-
core asphalt action!

The Ollie

You need to have this skill in the bag if you
want to do a whole load of the more advanced
scooter moves. The Ollie is *the* best way to
get some air without the aid of curbs, steps
or, specially-designed ramps. And if you can
get air, you can jump your scoot on to, over,
and off just about anything. So if you were
wondering which trick to learn first, this is
most definitely the one!

You should try practicing it on the spot
to begin with. Then, as you start to get
more height, you can give it a go in
motion. Each time you get it right, you'll go
a little higher. After a while, the only thing
keeping you on Earth will be the trick-
rider's arch enemy – gravity!

Q The Trick

Start off by carefully positioning your feet. Your back foot should be near the back of the deck, with the heel raised and your weight centered on the ball and toes. Your front foot should be near the head of the scoot, and angled forward.

Make sure you are comfortable with the balance, then push down with your back foot. Right away jump up, leading with your back foot and follow with your front foot after sliding it right to the front of the deck. (This probably sounds complicated, but it's just about working out the timing. Once you get that figured out, you WILL be hooked!)

When you jump, pull the handlebars with you, that way you'll gain more height. Then, while you're in the air, bend your legs and relax your arms. Doing this helps to cushion your body ready to absorb the landing.

And that's it! You've completed your first scoot trick. The only extra thing you have to learn, if you want to pull off the perfect Ollie mid-glide, is how to land and continue scooting smoothly. Once you've got that sorted, you can start using the Ollie to clear obstacles or jump curbs and steps. And there's only one way to get that dialed: Lots of practice ... and probably a bruised butt!

Ollie Manual

Want to do wheelies on your scoot? Then you're gonna love this!

The Ollie Manual is the next step up from a basic Ollie. It looks great and will help you develop balance and control over your scooter when doing stunts.

Q The Trick

To pull off the Ollie Manual, you need to be cruising at a good speed, so set yourself scooting with some strong, firm kicks. Then, do a normal Ollie, but try to land on the back wheel only. Pull on the handlebars to keep the front of the scoot in the air and wheelie down the sidewalk as far as you can before grounding it. WooooooHooooooo!

Three things will help you get it right:

✛ Positioning your feet so you can balance over the back wheel (but without pressing on the brake).

✛ Arcing your body forward toward the handlebars.

✛ Keeping the handlebars raised as high as you comfortably can off the ground (Not easy, but so, so rad when you get it dialed!).

One way to get good at this trick is to chalk some marks on the ground and challenge yourself to wheelie that distance. Don't give up till you can do it several times

If you want to use the Ollie Manual to jump a curb, a top tip is to not Ollie too high. You want your scoot's back end to be just high enough to clear the curb. That way you can slam the rear-wheel down straight away and begin wheelie-ing while you still have lots of speed. (The slower you are moving, the harder it will be to balance.)

in a row. You really want to be hot at this. The Streetstyler wants you to be able to Ollie Manual in your *sleep*! Getting it nailed will make loads of the complicated tricks a whole lot easier.

180º

After Ollies, this is definitely the next most useful trick to have under your belt. It's also the best and coolest-looking way to change direction while you're scooting. You do it by Ollie-ing and using your body-weight to spin the scooter around in the air. The idea is to end up facing the opposite way to where you started.

Like most of the tricks, it's a lot harder than it sounds, and a lot of people have real problems getting enough turn on their jumps. If you only manage a 45° to start with, don't worry, you are still looking good! And remember that the more you twist your body, the more momentum you will get.

Q The Trick

Bend your legs into the Ollie position and jump as high as you can. As soon as you take off, turn your shoulders and upper-body to the left or the right. (The Streetstyler recommends turning to the right if you are right-handed and to the left if you are left-handed.) As long as you keep a really tight grip on the handlebars, the scoot should turn and spin with you through the air. As you land, bend and relax your body like you would to complete a normal Ollie.

It will take you a while to learn how far to

turn your shoulders. To begin with, your turns will probably be too little or too big. With practice, knowing how far to twist your body will start to come naturally, and you will have learned one of the most useful stunts of all.

BunnyHop

Ever watched trials biking? Those riders do this stunt a lot, and it's pretty simple as long as your sense of balance is OK. It's a bit like doing an Ollie Manual, except you start from a standing position, and "hop" without the back wheel turning (instead of letting it glide you along).

Q The Trick

All you have to do is slide both feet toward the rear of the scoot, so that your right foot is over the brake and your weight is balanced over the back wheel. Then you pull up the handlebar to a 45° angle, and "hop" the scoot along by jumping and landing on the back wheel.

It's not the *most* impressive trick in the world, but it's great for jumping your scoot up curbs, or over cracks in the sidewalk. And it starts to look very cool if you use it as part of a larger tricks routine, or do something a little different with it. Try doing a series of hops – or even backward hops – if you want to grab some attention.

TailTwitch

This trick gives you pretty much the same results as an Ollie. The only difference is that you get to show off more!

Imagine there is an obstacle on the sidewalk and you're scooting straight at it. You could leap off your scoot, or whizz around the outside. But wouldn't it be cool to make like you were gonna Ollie over it, then, at the last second – while you're airborne – push the scoot's tail out to 45° ... and bring it back again before you land! The Streetstyler can already see the jaws dropping on those passers-by! Oh YEAH! OW! OW! OW!!!

The key to bagging it is being shifty-quick with your footwork – and keeping your back foot against the brake so that the deck can't get away from you. You could practice with an imaginary obstacle to begin with – otherwise you'll just keep spilling!

Q The Trick

 First up, you need to get enough speed going to complete the move. As you get close to your "target," push back your rear foot so that it's to the back of the deck and squashed over the foot-brake. After just a moment, Ollie and bring the leg that's on the brake forward and to the right. Your momentum will shoot the deck out to the right too. Then, as you come back to earth, slide your foot back to its original position – your feet and the deck are facing forward. When you land, either ease off the brake to continue scooting, or keep it hammered down to make a sliding stop.

Try combining it with an Ollie Manual landing if you're feeling really cocky!

CurbRide

This move's a real crowd-pleaser when you're cruising the streets. And it's one of those tricks where you'll be glad you learned the Ollie and the 180°.

The idea is to jump on to a curb, planting the scoot's nose and front wheel over the edge, then jump back off while spinning to perform a 180° so you land facing away from the curb.

It's best to practice this one on a low curb to start with – one that you can Ollie quite easily.

Q The Trick

Cruise on up to it, then Ollie so that you land facing on to the sidewalk, with half the deck on the curb and half off. Be sure to have your weight slightly toward the front of the scoot – otherwise you will ground the deck and either slide off, or be totally unable to do the second part of the trick.

Next up, Ollie back off the curb, twisting your body as you would for a normal 180°.

Hopefully you will land facing away from the curb and ready to ride off into the arms of your adoring fans!

Like a lot of the tricks, you can do a bunch of variations with this move. One cool option is to twist further and go for a 270° (a three-quarter turn). That way you will land right alongside the side-walk, which looks real smooth. It's very easy to have a BIG, messy spill practicing this though! So the Streetstyler recommends you only do it in front of your close mates till you are totally sure you have it dialed!

Learning these moves will give you plenty of ammunition to impress your mates. Not only that, they're a totally excellent launch-pad into the world of really complex scoot trickery. But before you get to that, have some of this...

Before you try out the next batch of awesomely complicated tricks and stunts, take a breather and check out Phantom Ollie's low-down on personalizing and modifying your scoot. They will totally inspire you to grab some huge air!! AROOOOOWWW!!!!!

Hi guys. The Streetstyler has asked me to talk to you about making your scooter look a little different. I guess because I have a pretty rad one. It's based on my favorite movie, *The Phantom Menace.* That's how I got my nickname too.

Modifying your scooter is easy and a lot of fun. You can cover the frame in stickers, or spray-paint designs on it. You can even bolt on some specially-made accessories that the manufacturers and designers have started making.

Handle-grips

One of the simplest things to change is the handle-grips. Most scoots come with black grips which you can pull off quite easily, and swap for all sorts of rad colors – like blues, reds, and crazy fluros. I even saw one girl with brown furry ones! She probably made those herself though. All you would need is some fabric, scissors and a strong glue.

Deck-grips

The deck-grip is simple to replace too. Your scoot normally comes with the company's logo as a deck-grip. These look pretty cool, but if you want something unique, you can quickly peel and scrub it off with warm, soapy water. I got a special *Phantom Menace* grip online, and there's all kinds of other crazy stuff around, like leopard prints or zebra stripes. If you're going to make your own, just remember to choose something with a non-slippy surface – the deck-grip is supposed to help you stay on the scoot!

Wheels

The wheels are designed to be replaced easily. That's coz they wear out if you scoot a lot. New ones come in all different colors. I have one blue and one fluro-orange, but you can get pretty much any combination. Having different colors looks cool when you go fast.

LEDs

But not as cool as fitting LEDs! This is one of the gnarliest add-ons you can buy for a scoot. LEDs are little red lights that snap onto your deck-plate and are completely motion-sensitive. That means they only flash when you are in action. And they look totally rad when you're doing tricks! You can get light-up wheels too, but they aren't so cool, coz they cost more than normal ones, and you still have to replace them as often.

Bearings

Another easy thing to change is your scoot's wheel-bearings. Your machine will most likely come with fairly standard ones, so if you upgrade, you'll get a noticeably smoother and slightly faster ride. Bearings are rated on smoothness using a measurement called ABEC. The smoother a bearing is, the better it will work. The best bearings are ABEC 7. The worst are ABEC 1. Anything over ABEC 3 is cool for scooters, but if you want to race, or do tricks, go for something a bit higher. You can buy kits that include a set of ABEC 5s, spacers (to keep the bearings at an equal distance), and an Allen key to fit them. If you're not sure about fitting them yourself, someone in a skate shop should be able to help.

You'll probably need some shop-hints for a few other upgrades too. One popular one is to fix a BMX-style handbrake to the handlebars. You definitely get improved stopping power with one of these, but it's hard to fit it yourself without leaving the brake-cable flapping around – especially when you try to fold the scoot. This can be a little dangerous coz you could get caught up in it when you wipe-out. So get some help.

Steering Columns

It's also possible to change your steering column for one that ends with a suspended front-wheel fork – very cool for tricksters, and I've even seen some scoots where the single wheel at the front or back has been replaced with a set of two in-line-style ones! It looks cool, and will definitely improve speed and balance, but it's probably not one to try yourself. Oll's advice? Seek professional help!

Grindplates

One add-on you can fit yourself is a grindplate (also called a kickplate). This is great if you're into trickwork, coz it will help protect the bottom of your scoot. It fits underneath the deck, and attaches to the foot-brake and just behind the front-wheel. You can get them in a load of different styles and colors. I have a silver one with a *Star Wars* Confederation emblem.

Trick-pegs

Trick-pegs can be a great addition for stunt-riding too. At the moment, you have to get specially-made wheels that have a connection point for the pegs to slide into, but there should soon be scoot wheels ready-designed with pegs attached. I've only seen a couple of people with them fitted so far, but they are totally worth having because you can do a lot more tricks. Especially if you mount them on the front and back wheels!

Bag It!

And the best accessory of all? This one you can have without making any changes to your scoot! It's a specially-designed carry sack, so that you can sling the scooter over your shoulder when you're not using it. Most of the scoot-makers sell them, but it's pretty easy to make your own. You just sew a tube of fabric and add a handle. Mine's light-blue, like Qui-Gon's lightsabre! There are also special backpacks you can buy now that have an extended pocket to slide your scoot into. These are pretty cool if you ride your scoot to school – you can keep it separate from your books so they don't get messed up.

These tricks are a little harder than those you've already tried. Most can be done anywhere, so long as you have flat ground and some curbing. But for the ones toward the end of the chapter, you will need a miniramp. They come in all shapes and sizes and you can buy them in most skate shops. Or you could try making your own. Just look for a smooth, flat piece of board – either wood, or metal – and some blocks to prop it up securely at one end.

Ramps vary a lot in height. The Streetstyler's advice is to start on a small one and work your way up. Landing a scoot – especially a two-wheeler – after a jump is NOT easy.

Grinds

Any time you Ollie up and slide along a surface using, a part of your scoot other than the wheels, you are grinding. And it's music to the Streetstyler's ears! There's nothing like the sound of a scoot gliding along a curb, rail, step, or ledge. MMMM-MMMM!!!!!!

Make sure you fit a grindplate if you want to try this type of trick – otherwise you're gonna get through a lot of scoot decks!

DeckSlide

This is the most common type of grind, and the one you should learn first. It's a trick that will help you get the feel of how your scoot slides along different obstacles (curb, rail, wooden box, low-wall, what ever). It's also a safe-ish way to test if an obstacle is slidable, before you attack it with a more complicated piece of trickery!

Q The Trick

The Streetstyler's method is to cruise toward the obstacle at about 45°, then, when we get to about 30cm away, spring an Ollie.

From that distance, you should be able to land with half the deck on, and half off the obstacle.

Land facing straight up onto the sidewalk. Center your weight and let your momentum sliiiiiiiiiiiiide you along.

The slide will last longer if you shift your weight back and forth on the scoot – this will help you keep your balance too. When you hit that point where you're about to lose your balance coz the scoot has slowed so much (or you are running out of obstacle!), turn the scoot through at least 45°. Not too much more though, you don't want the wheels to snag the obstacle coz that'll spill you. Then Ollie back off, making sure you get at least a 90° turn to be sure of a clean clearance.

If you don't find this totally addictive, the Streetstyler is gonna be truly amazed! In fact, we reckon as soon as you master it, you'll want to try the **SlantedGrind**. For this one, all you do differently is land the deck on the curb or rail at a slight angle – something like 45°. It's a little more challenging coz it's harder to maintain momentum this way. And remember that because the scoot is angled, you will probably need to twist it a little when you come to Ollie off.

You could also try the **SlantedGrind 180°**. This time, as you approach the curb, pull a 180° so that you land and grind facing backward! This one not only looks way cool, it's great if you need to make a quick getaway – you're already facing the path to freedom!

Rodeo 180°

The Streetstyler reckons we can see where whoever named this trick was coming from – coz it's a little like doing a bareback ride...

It's a stunt you can perform standing still or on the move, and the idea is to spin your scooter through 180° using only the back wheel. To do this right, you have to use your body weight to spin the scooter, and then try to shift your balance onto the back wheel so that the scoot's front end stays up throughout the turn.

Q The Trick

Place your right foot over the brake and back wheel, then slide your left foot down the scoot to nestle against it. Next, gripping the handlebar firmly in your left hand, raise your right hand away from your body – like a rodeo rider! OK, you might *feel* a little stupid, but it's the only way you will be able to balance during the trick.

Now you're in position, spin your body quickly so it moves around and away from the scoot. As long as you keep a good grip on the handlebars, they should turn with you – till they are parallel to your body. Meanwhile, the momentum of your turn should carry the scoot through a half-circle – so long as you can stay balanced on that back wheel (the difficult part!). Once you've spun, slide your foot back down the deck and re-balance on two wheels.

And if you can do that one while surfing along, the Streetstyler will be seriously impressed! But don't get too cocky. As soon as you have the 180° in the bag, you should try the...

Rodeo 360°

To pocket this stunt, you do the same moves as with a 180°, but coz you are going twice as far, you will need to spin your body *much* faster and be *even* more carefully balanced.

This is one of the Streetstyler's all-time

favorite tricks. And if you can pull it off in motion (which requires a *lot* of speed), the Rodeo 360° looks absolutely awesome. People watching will think, Yeah, I can do that. But then their brains will figure through all you have to do to get it dialed, and they'll be going: Whoaaaaaaaa! and drooling like dogs!!!

X-Up

This trick is based on an old BMX classic. It's a simple idea that works just as well on flat ground or in a pipe at a skatepark. You get some air, then turn the scooter's handlebars through 180° *and* back again before landing. No worries!

Q The Trick

First, glide up to a good cruising speed and get ready to Ollie. As soon as you leave the ground, pull the right handlebar upward, and push the left downward. You'll know when you've pushed the front wheel through 180° because your arms will cross (forming an X-shape). As soon as that happens, twist the bars back to the starting position ready to land in the same way you would for a normal Ollie... And milk the applause!

This stunt is a lot trickier than it sounds. If you have trouble getting it dialed, don't worry. It took the Streetstyler weeks to get right. And there *is* an easier way: The T-Up. All you do is grip the handlebars at their central point, and twist from there. You still get a 180°, it's just a tiny bit less awesome...

If you do get to grips with a full-on X-Up, try landing with your arms still crossed. That's so tough it might even earn a little respect from Chloe.

Yeah, if you can do it with both feet off the board too!

Nose Wheelie

This is another trick that comes to scooting from the world of BMX-ing. Like the X-up, it sounds simple, and looks great, but can be tricky to pull off. It might seem like the reverse of the Ollie Manual, but it's definitely harder!

If you have one of the newest model scoots with a built-in front-brake, then this is your lucky day. You should be able to perform this one pretty easily – just lock that brake and lean into it. For the rest of us, it's gonna take a lot of practice, because we will be relying totally on balance.

A good tip for getting the move together is to practice on grass. That way the front wheel sinks into the ground slightly and you can start to get a feel for where to position your body to keep from falling.

Q The Trick

First, you need to get a good grip on the handlebars, then slide your body-weight toward the front of the scooter. It might help you to rest your side against the handlebars to help maintain balance. That won't win you many prizes for technique, but it'll get the trick done.

As your weight moves down the scoot,

you will feel the back wheel begin to rise.

The trick is to find the point where you are balanced with the back end quite high off the ground, but so that you haven't slid too far forward that the scoot can shoot out from under you.

It's the kind of trick that doesn't look that impressive to people who don't ride scoots, so you should only pop it when you are with those in the know. They will see how much you've sweated to get it right and give you the cred you deserve. Especially if you start hopping on that front wheel too!!

TailWhip

TailWhips (sometimes called PopTail-Shovelts) are just about the trickiest stunt you can pull without ramps or pipes also one of the few tricks that can't attempted on a skateboard, bike or inlines. Yep – TailWhips are unique to scooter riders! And they are definitely worth all the effort (and bruises!) of learning. The TailWhip is amazing to watch – especially if you do it like it comes easy to you. That'll get you *maximum* respect from your fellow riders!

The basic idea is to Ollie, then spin the scoot's deck right out from under you and through 360° while your body is still airborne. You touch down on the deck again just as it completes its spin. Simple, right?!!!

Well... Maybe not. Which is why it's a cool idea to learn the Semi-TailWhip first. For this stunt, the Streetstyler says it's OK for your feet to touch the ground! And, like the other complicated tricks, you should try this one on the spot before attempting it in motion – unless you live for road rash! Landing on a spinning deck is HARD!

| Ollie | Spin that deck! | Back on deck! |

Q The Trick

Keeping your right foot on the scoot, place your left on the ground so that it's parallel to the front wheel. This foot will act as your pivot. Just as you plant it, flick the tail of the scoot with your right foot so that it spins away real fast in an anti-clockwise direction.

Keep a tight grip on the handlebars so they don't turn with the rest of the scoot, and the deck should shoot right round in front of you, spinning back toward your left side. As it completes its circuit, jump your left leg back up and on to the board – and try to make a steady landing!

Once you've got it dialed – and it does take time – try and pull it off in motion. The trick here is getting a good swift gliding speed, and kicking the board out fast enough that it comes back round before your legs are stretched all over the sidewalk!! Get that in the bag and you are ready to try for the absolute MUTHA!

Because you don't touch the ground at all with a full TailWhip it can seem almost impossible to perform. The Streetstyler reckons you solve this by breaking the stunt down into sections. When you've got your head round each part, try and execute them together.

Q The Trick

Start off by practicing flicking the deck around with your feet. Then practice the landing – which shouldn't be too hard if you can already do the Semi-TailWhip.

To do the full trick, bend your legs as if you were going to Ollie. As you spring up, flick your feet out to either the right or left to make the deck spin away from under you. Hold the handlebars tight, otherwise the scoot will spin off down the street. If you've timed it right, the scoot's deck should spin through 180° just as you reach the top point of your jump, completing its circuit just as your feet come down. Then all you have to do is hit the deck and land like you would for an Ollie.

Ramp Jumps

If you want to ramp jump on a scooter, there's one thing you need a lot of: SPEED! You should place your ramp at the bottom of a steep hill, or use a launch ramp to build up enough momentum. (If you live somewhere flat, check to see if your skatepark has ramp facilities before you think about buying two ramps!!). Don't attempt ramp-tricks unless you are sure of a lot of speed. It's just too dangerous. You'll either tip right off the end of your ramp, or fade mid-jump and end up smeared all across the floor. So, before you try the ramp, do a few test-runs alongside it to make sure you sail on a good distance.

One Footer

This is the best one to learn first as it's all about just jumping and landing with confidence, and getting the feel of ramp-work in preparation for harder stunts. You don't even have to jump that high with One Footers. And no one will point and laugh if your leg doesn't make it back on to the deck before you land. As long as you get from the start of the jump to the end in one piece, you're a success!

Q The Trick

To pull it off, race toward the ramp at a good speed (you will soon get to know what kind of pace you need to do good jumps) and clear the ramp. When you reach the highest point of your leap, kick out one of your feet to the left or right hand side. (It MUST be to the side, otherwise you will unbalance and wipe-out HUGELY.) Hold your foot out for as long as you comfortably can, then try to bring it back to the deck before you land.

The first time you try this, you'll probably only manage a super-fast little flick-kick, and it'll seem impossible to do any more. But as you get used to the feel of being in the air with only one foot on the deck you will be able to hold it out there longer and longer. Then you can try...

Can-Can

This trick is named after a crazy dance invented in France coz it uses sort of the same leg movements. You don't have to wear a frilly dress to do it (unless you really want to!). The trick can be performed in several different ways, but the one you'll see tricksters attempting most often is called the One-Footed Can-Can.

Q The Trick

To get it dialed, head for the ramp at a good jumping speed. As you take the jump, do the smallest of One-Footers off to the side. It doesn't really need to be a kick, just enough movement for your foot to leave the deck. Then bring your foot across the deck and kick it out very slightly to the otherside (strangely, it's not as hard as it sounds!). To complete the move, kick back to the original position and bring your foot to rest on the deck again as you land.

For your first few attempts, you probably won't manage to complete the move, but you'll be freaked by how much you can move your legs about in the short time you're in the air! Once you've realized that, the Streetstyler reckons you'll be trying all kinds of crazy variations.

One Hander

Trying to take a hand off the handlebars mid-jump is harder than lifting a foot in midair. Probably because you *think* you are

gonna accidentally twist the steering column – even if you *know* you won't! And
once you've done a few jumps, you'll know
that it can be very bad when that happens.

Q The Trick

Head toward the ramp at your
normal, comfortable jumping
speed. Decide before you launch
into the air which hand you are
going to lift clear of the grip. It's probably
best to keep your stronger hand on the
handlebars for the first few tries. You won't
be quite so nervous about letting your
weaker hand do the flapping about!

Just before you reach the highest point in
your jump, release the handlebar. The first
time you try it, it's a good idea to just relax
your hold on the grip, but keep your hand
resting on it. It'll give you more confidence
for your next run. As you land, close your
hand back around the grip.

It'll probably take you quite a few tries to
become comfortable with even moving
your hand a tiny bit away from the handle-

bar, but with enough practice you will be moving it a good distance – maybe even waving to your fans down on the ground!!

No Footer

If you like your tricks burly, this is one for you! You need to be very confident with all the other ramp moves before you even think about attempting the No Footer.

Q The Trick

Cruise up the ramp at your normal jumping speed and launch out. At the highest point of your jump, pull both your feet off the deck and kick them out to the sides. You need to be perfectly balanced to do this, and you must be sure that your steering column is attached properly, coz it's gonna be taking all your weight.

As with the One-Footer and the Can-Can, your kicks don't have to be huge – you will be able to go bigger the more you practice. You MUST get both feet back onto the board before you land though. The Streetstyler doesn't want to think about what will happen to your knees otherwise. YEEEOOOOU-UUCHHH!!!

There are *hundreds* more stunts and variations of stunts you can do on your scooter, and we're gonna show you a whole load more of them in chapter eleven. So, get out there and practice, practice, practice. And repeat after the Streetstyler: I can do this trick. I CAN do this trick. I CAN DO THIS TRICK!!!

And that's it. Once you've learned all these, you should throw away your scoot, coz there's nothing left to learn. **JUST KIDDING!**

Are We Gonna Have A Problem Here...? 10

If you've got a scoot problem, if no one else can help and if you can find him, maybe you should ask the Dek Doktor.

Yeah, maybe you should.

Let's take a shifty through his bulging post-bag:

I just bought a Kickboard and it's really wobbly. Is something wrong with the wheels?

Troy (Seattle)

Could be. But ride it a few times anyhow – it may be the rider, not the scoot.

Hi Dok! I have an old Micro that used to be my bros. When I Ollie it sounds like it's gonna break. Should I get a new one?

Burly Paul (Houston)

Tricky one. It takes a lot to break a scoot, but the older ones do weaken in the end – especially around the rear axle. Keep on using it. If all you're doing is Ollies, the worst that'll happen is a break. Then you should retire the scoot with full honors! Don't use it for more than that though. No point in taking stupid chances! Get a new scoot with suspension for tougher tricks.

Doc,
The Streetstyler says when you wheelie on your front wheel it's a Nose Wheelie. I always thought it was a Hang Ten. Who's right?

Krazy Rob (Glasgow)

 Both of you. Tricks have lots of different names. It mostly depends on where you come from. Some tricks change their names because they become recognized as a particular scoot-head's trademark. Maybe one day the Nose Wheelie will be called Krazy's Nose!

Dear Dek Doktor,
My brake squeaks really bad on hills. How do I stop this?

Marisa (NewYork)

Check that the brake and the wheel are both free of grit and dirt, and make sure the wheel is tightened properly. If the wheel runs straight and free of dirt, you shouldn't have a squeak problem.

Dek,
I know this guy with really dumb hair. It's really short at the front and sides, but really long at the back. Is this a mullet?

KT_90 (London)

Yes!

116

Dear Doktor,
If I make changes to my scooter and then it gets broken, will the manufacturer still replace it?

Jon (Denmark)

 That totally depends on the changes you make. If you use products that your scoot-maker officially endorses, then they will replace the scooter if it breaks due to a design or build fault. But... If you make any other modifications – even a new paint job! – you might be canceling your warranty.

Hi! I just got a scooter and I want to put different color wheels and ABEC bearings on, but I can't get the old wheels off. What do I do?

Corsten (Munich)

117

It can be hard to find the right-sized Allen key to remove your wheels. If you tried already with one that wasn't the right size, you may have threaded the head. Take your scoot to a skate shop and let the pros sort it out! One good thing – once you replace the wheels, you will get the right size Allen key coz most packs come with one included.

Dok,
I saw some guy with these weird curved side-plates screwed onto his deck. What are they for?

Carla (Maine)

Some people have started widening their decks with "wings." It's a simple modification that most skate shops can do for you. Wings

118

help stabilize the scooter, making tricks easier because they leave more room for your feet.

Dek,
I think I saw Brad Pitt and Jennifer Aniston riding a Razor. Was it them?   Lisa Marie (Illinois)

How would I know?
I'm the Dek Doktor,
not a celebrity
stalker.

Dear Dr,
My mom says I can't have a scooter because they are too dangerous. She says thousands of kids have cut off their fingers trying to unfold their scooters. Is she right?
Matt (Oxford)

It's true that people get hurt riding scoots but no more than they do from joining in any other sport. Your mom should chill a little – as long as you are wearing the right safety gear. However, some scooters have been recalled as they have sharp edges on the steering column that you only see when you are folding your scooter. The Dok recomends sanding any sharp edges as soon as you get your scoot. Most scoots already have this done, but checking hurts a lot less than a severed finger tip!

This section is for those of you who want to follow in the footsteps of the pros.

You won't find any easy stunts on these pages. They're called tricks coz they are well TRICKY. But, if you put in the practice, the Streetstyler just knows you will get 'em dialed. There are *not* a lot of scoot-riders out there who can pull off all these big-time crowd-pleasers.

TECH-TALK!

Concave = A tranny that arcs inward.
Convex = A tranny that arcs outward.
Coping = Any grindable and slidable material attached to an obstacle to make grinds and slides easier. Most commonly found at the top end of trannys such as half-pipes.
Half-Pipe = A specially-made ramp with concave transitions at each end.
Transition = (Tranny) = Any surface for skating that isn't totally horizontal

> or vertical – anything from the
> slightest dip or hump to a fully
> concave pipe.

Most of these stunts can be done any-where. But for a few, you need to visit a skatepark and get yourself onto a transi-tion. If you're up for giving that a go, choose a park where the equipment is in good order, there is some kind of supervision, and you have access to a phone. Scoot injuries in skateparks are rare, but they can happen. So it's good that you're wearing all your safeties, right? Right! Then let's BURNNNNNNNNNN!!!

DropIn

This is a little move for making a stylish entry into a concave transition like a half-pipe. It's simple, but scary, coz you are basically hurling yourself and your scoot out off a precipice! If you've not tried this kind of transition before, you should ride it a few times without doing stunts to get used to the weird feeling.

Done that? Cool. Let's Droooop Innnnn!!!

Q The Trick

Position the scooter so that its front third is right out over the coping. Keep your back foot onboard – and on the brake – to prevent the scooter from tipping into the pipe too soon. Take a good deep breath (!) and step your other foot forward onto the deck, and grab the handlebars, crouching low over the scoot, so it and your body will tilt down into the transition together.

Make sure you lean a long way forward and are *determined* to complete the trick. If you hesitate or panic, the deck can shoot out from under you – even if you're gripping the handlebars firmly. You really don't want that to happen. No sir.

But don't lean *too* far. You'll end up plunging down the transition ahead of your scooter – probably collecting the handlebars in your gut along the way! You don't want that to happen either. No sireeeeeee.

The bad news is... Unless you're really lucky, you will only know the right distance to lean by wiping out a few times. Well, hey... The Streetstyler never told you these moves would be easy!

Rock'N'Roll

To complete this trick you first need to have enough speed to reach the coping at the top of the transition. You can kick back and forth in the pipe to build up that kind of speed, or use the momentum you already have from another trick like the DropIn.

Q The Trick

When your scoot reaches the coping, get your front wheel and part of the deck over the edge. Then quickly lean in with your front foot so you are rocking back and forth, balanced on the coping. And that's the easy part! Now you have to switch your weight into an Ollie-ing position and perform a 180°. The trick here is clearing the coping with your wheels as you turn. Otherwise you'll make a big scootery mess all the way down the pipe! If you do manage the turn, slip straight into the DropIn move and scoot back down the transition ready to receive the Streetstyler Medal of Maximum Respect!!!

50-50

For this move you need to combine good pipe-work with grinding skills you've already learned. Before you try it, you need to get to grips with stalling your scoot up on the coping. That way you can get your head around how to balance on the lip of the tranny – an essential part of pulling off a good grind.

Q The Trick

Work up some speed so that you can race head-on to the top of the transition. As your front wheel clears the coping, flick the back end of the scoot into an angled slide so that it spins through 90°. Then try to balance on the lip of the tranny without toppling. (The first few times you will probably have to put your foot down for support.) When you have this dialed, you can try for the grind.

Head up that transition with some serious speed. Make sure you are at an angle too – otherwise you'll fly straight out of the pipe! As your front wheel clears the lip of the tranny, spin the back end of the scoot almost as far as you would to stall, but not enough that the back wheel clears the coping. Then lean your weight forward and toward the coping, and let your momentum glide you along in a SERIOUS grinding action! Oh, and don't forget to spin into a DropIn before you run out of pipe!

Grabs

You're doing one of these anytime you

reach down and grasp your deck while in the air. But guess what...? Grabs are *hard* on a scooter! The "easiest" way to do them is to crouch low and reach for the deck-plate just in front of your front foot. Be careful of the deck wheel – the Streetstyler doesn't want to see anyone get their fingers mashed! Try your first grabs when you're Ollie-ing on flat ground. When you get used to the action, give it a try on a transition.

Q The Trick

Take it easy and go up the slope at only a slight angle. If you try to carve into it big-style, all you'll end up doing is sailing to the ground while your scoot flies off over the coping. So... aim small till you've got control!

As you near the top of the curve, you should begin to reach for the scoot's deck so that when your front wheel clears the coping, your hand will be closing for the grab. Then as your back wheel hits the coping, put the slightest pressure on your back foot. This will help bring the deck into your hand, as well as send you in the right direction – UP!

This is The Streetstyler Signing Off!

The world of scooters is movin' on up, changing, and transforming all the time. The Streetstyler may have said our piece, but we reckon there will be a million and one more things to say in a few months from now – and you will be a part of it! Already we hear rumors of a new generation of scooters that are gonna blow your minds.

We've still got a couple of spaces in our posse – if we can find anyone good enough to fill them. So we're gonna be out there, watching all you guys. Practice enough, and you could be riding with us. Shoulder to shoulder.   **Peace...**

It's getting real misty outside...